Managing Your Whole Life

IDEAS INTO ACTION GUIDEBOOKS

Aimed at managers and executives who are concerned with their own and others' development, each guidebook in this series gives specific advice on how to complete a developmental task or solve a leadership problem.

LEAD CONTRIBUTORS	Marian N. Ruderman, Phillip W. Braddy, Kelly M. Hannum
SPECIAL CONTRIBUTOR	Ellen E. Kossek
CONTRIBUTORS	Dawn Barts, Anand Chandrasekar, Craig Chappelow, Kim Leahy, Jean Leslie, Bertrand Sereno, Hughes Van Stichel, Sophia Zhao
DIRECTOR OF ASSESSMENTS, TOOLS, AND PUBLICATIONS	Sylvester Taylor
MANAGER, PUBLICATION DEVELOPMENT	Peter Scisco
EDITORS	Stephen Rush, Karen Lewis
ASSOCIATE EDITOR	Shaun Martin
COPY EDITOR	Tazmen Hansen
DESIGN AND LAYOUT	Joanne Ferguson
COVER DESIGN	Laura J. Gibson Chris Wilson, 29 & Company
RIGHTS AND PERMISSIONS	Kelly Lombardino

CCL No. 458
ISBN No. 978-1-60491-162-6

CENTER FOR CREATIVE LEADERSHIP
WWW.CCL.ORG

AN IDEAS INTO ACTION GUIDEBOOK

Managing Your Whole Life

Marian N. Ruderman, Phillip W. Braddy, Kelly M. Hannum, and Ellen E. Kossek

Center for
Creative
Leadership®

THE IDEAS INTO ACTION GUIDEBOOK SERIES

This series of guidebooks draws on the practical knowledge that the Center for Creative Leadership (CCL) has generated since its inception in 1970. The purpose of the series is to provide leaders with specific advice on how to complete a developmental task or solve a leadership challenge. In doing that, the series carries out CCL's mission to advance the understanding, practice, and development of leadership for the benefit of society worldwide.

CCL's unique position as a research and education organization supports a community of accomplished scholars and educators in a community of shared knowledge. CCL's knowledge community holds certain principles in common, and its members work together to understand and generate practical responses to the ever-changing circumstances of leadership and organizational challenges.

In its interactions with a richly varied client population, in its research into the effect of leadership on organizational performance and sustainability, and in its deep insight into the workings of organizations, CCL creates new, sound ideas that leaders all over the world put into action every day. We believe you will find the Ideas Into Action Guidebooks an important addition to your leadership toolkit.

Table of Contents

IN BRIEF

Managing work-life boundaries is essential for optimizing productivity and effectiveness at work and at home. Blurring or otherwise not successfully managing these boundaries can lead to a variety of problems, such as mistakes at work, decreased organizational coordination, and increased stress and tension. Successful leaders use a variety of techniques to approach their whole life, including setting clear boundaries, utilizing effective time management, managing transitions between work and family roles, and using goals as a means to organize their lives. To understand your current work-life situation, you must analyze your behaviors (what you're currently doing), your identity (where you prefer to invest your time and energy), and your perceived control (your ability to decide when, where, and how to take care of work and family responsibilities). Combining data from these three categories, you can come up with a comprehensive development plan that will allow you to achieve your goals at home and at work, leading to a successful, fulfilling life.

Navigating the Work-Life Divide

Just as the industrial age introduced separation between work and family time, the information age has given us the means to integrate work and family roles. Many of us can work anywhere and anytime, and can connect with or attend to family and friends anywhere and anytime. And increasingly, we are doing both. When we are with family and friends, we check for communications from work. When we are at work, we check for messages from family members.

In this guidebook, we do not argue that the blurring of work-life boundaries is a good or bad thing. However, we do acknowledge those blurred lines and recognize that individuals

have greater say over their personal boundaries than was previously possible. There is no evidence of one best way to manage boundaries between work and personal life. Instead, research by the Center for Creative Leadership (conducted in partnership with Dr. Ellen Ernst Kossek, the Basil S. Turner Professor of Management at Purdue University and coauthor of *CEO of Me: Creating a Life That Works in the Flexible Job Age*) shows there are many ways to successfully manage these boundaries. In fact, our research links several different boundary-management styles or preferences to a variety of meaningful outcomes, including lower work-life conflict, increased workplace retention, engagement, and enhanced psychological well-being.

Because boundaries can be a sensitive topic in the context of organizations and families, we suggest ways to think and talk about managing boundaries that make the process visible and discussable. We also describe a set of concepts that can raise your appreciation of boundary management, setting the stage for you to improve your boundary-management techniques. Managing work-life boundaries does not need to be difficult. If you take time to periodically reflect on and discuss your preferences with others in a nondefensive way and are proactive in managing boundaries with work and family stakeholders, you can create a healthier, more productive, and less stressful life.

In the following pages, you will find a process that will help you understand your preferences for managing work-life boundaries. Armed with that understanding, you can use this guidebook's suggested practices to regain control over your life.

The Importance of Managing Work-Life Boundaries

Blurred boundaries can contribute to your well-being and the well-being of your organization and your family, but you must deal with trade-offs. On the positive side, the blurring of work-life boundaries makes life easier. Being constantly accessible can make a dramatic difference in the speed at which things get done. You no longer need to be face-to-face to connect and interact with colleagues or family members. It is a great boost to productivity to have information available from a mobile device. Being able to work outside an office creates tremendous freedom, cuts down on travel, and frees people to work when and where they choose. It also reduces unscheduled absences due to personal issues and may increase productivity.

On the negative side, these same boundary-blurring characteristics create the opportunity for us to interrupt one another at almost any time. As a result, many leaders are pulled in multiple directions and cannot focus on the situations they are in at the moment. Extensive interruptions can have profound implications, such as the following:

- shallow, hurried decision-making processes
- urgent, unimportant issues overshadowing important ones
- decreased focus on rapidly changing circumstances
- decreased coordination among team and unit members
- increased errors and mistakes from rushing
- psychological overload from increased cognitive complexity

People can become so busy responding to electronic devices and messages that they have little or no downtime at all, leading to increased stress and negative consequences for individuals and their organizations.

Individual Consequences

Many people worry that the constant blurring of boundaries allows work to intrude on their ability to raise a family or to have productive nonwork relationships. Healthy relationships require attention. In *Alone Together: Why We Expect More from Technology and Less from Each Other*, author Sherry Turkle explains the risk that high levels of connectivity pose to social relationships. Blurred boundaries pose implications for health because of the stress associated with constant contact, which can contribute to health problems such as hypertension and hyperglycemia.

9

Prolonged stress is also associated with impaired cognitive function and lowered energy levels. The way many busy people live challenges their capacity to remain resilient in the face of such stress. Time for rest, relaxation, and reflection is difficult to come by, but it is essential for building resilience.

Organizational Consequences

Some organizations don't see stress and related issues as their concern. However, leaders are stewards of the organization, and they should be concerned about the negative effects of stress and related issues. According to the National Institute for Occupational Safety and Health (NIOSH), a federal agency dedicated to researching workplace health and safety issues, stress at work is associated with employee absenteeism and turnover. If employees don't have time to concentrate and focus, how do you think that affects your organization's performance? What effect do interruptions that break concentration have on collaboration, innovation, and sustainability in your organization?

Connectivity is inherently neither good nor bad, but it becomes a problem when individuals and organizations allow it to take over work-life boundaries in a way that limits the effectiveness of organizational members. It's possible to create and navigate boundaries so that they nourish you rather than deplete you. Now it's time to learn how.

A New Approach for Managing Work-Life Boundaries

What can you do to take advantage of connectivity without being overthrown by the disadvantages? The answer begins with how you aim to fulfill the responsibilities of your work and personal relationships.

There are three important concepts that can help you understand how you currently manage the boundaries between your work and personal life:

1. Your behaviors: How do you manage work or family interruptions?

2. Your identity: Where do you prefer to invest your time and energy?

3. Your perceived control: How much control do you feel you have over how you fulfill your work- and family-related roles and responsibilities?

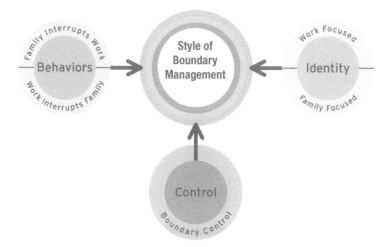

These three ideas support many different ways of managing the work-life boundary in response to the many different desires and ways that people have for handling work and personal time. In the following sections, you will learn about these diverse patterns. Additionally, you will find questions to use in considering how you manage work-life boundaries.

Behaviors

In general, people follow five basic behavioral patterns for organizing their work in the context of the rest of life:

Integrators blend work and personal tasks throughout their day. Their family and personal responsibilities interrupt work time, and their work responsibilities interrupt family time. For example, an Integrator may regularly schedule and attend family events (for example, a child's sporting event) during traditional work hours but may also take care of business e-mails, phone calls, and tasks while spending time with his or her family.

 Separators keep work and personal activities separate. They focus on work tasks while at work and focus on family activities while at home. They use physical space, schedules, and discipline to establish clear boundaries and protect both work and family time.

 Work Firsters let work activities interrupt family time but do not permit family activities to interrupt work. They focus primarily on job-related activities while at work and also take care of business e-mails, phone calls, and tasks during family time. Their schedules suggest that work time takes precedence over family time.

 Family Firsters permit family activities to interrupt work but typically do not allow work activities to interrupt family time. Although they may complete personal tasks during work time, they tend to focus exclusively on nonwork activities during personal time. Their schedules suggest that family time takes precedence over work time—the opposite of Work Firsters.

 Cyclers alternate between periods of integrating and separating work and family, choosing either separation or integration as needed to fulfill their obligations.

For example, tax accountants in the United States may separate work and family during the tax season (January through April) so they have long periods of time during the day to focus on their heavy workloads. After April, however, they may integrate work and family, intentionally taking more time during work to attend to family or personal needs.

No specific behavioral style is best for all individuals or across all situations. Each can elicit positive and negative perceptions in others. Exercise 1, Behavior, will help you determine which behavior style best fits your current work-life situation.

Identity

A second way of thinking about boundaries is in terms of identity. Your identity refers to how you see yourself and where you prefer to invest your time and energy. There are four identity types:

Work-Focused individuals are career oriented and primarily invest themselves in their work. They prefer to give their best energy to their job-related activities.

Family-Focused individuals primarily identify with a family role. They prefer to invest most of their energy in being a parent, grandparent, spouse, or caregiver.

Dual-Focused individuals invest time and energy equally in both work and family. They prefer to structure their time so that they can give their best to both domains.

Other-Focused individuals prefer to invest their time and energy in life interests that do not directly relate to work or family. For example, they may prefer to invest in community volunteering or in their hobbies.

Exercise 1: Behavior

Choose the behavior style that best describes you and also examine the associated perceptions others may have of your behavioral type. You can emphasize positive aspects of your behavioral style and manage negative perceptions to help others hold an accurate (and, one hopes, positive) view of your boundary-managing behavior.

Behavioral Type	Positive Perceptions	Negative Perceptions
❏ Integrators	They can do it all, they can multitask, and they are always available.	They appear to be exhausted; they are always in a hurry.
❏ Separators	They are reliable and professional.	They are rigid and are not adaptable.
❏ Work Firsters	They are dedicated and professional.	They work too much and are detached from their families.
❏ Family Firsters	They are dedicated to and protective of family.	They are rigid and self-centered.
❏ Cyclers	They are fully engaged and flexible.	Their lives are chaotic, and they often appear exhausted.

Blurred boundaries can contribute to your well-being and the well-being of your organization and your family, but you must deal with trade-offs.

Exercise 2, Identity, will help you determine your identity type. As with the five behaviors, there is not one superior identity type. Additionally, there are positive and negative perceptions others associate with each identity type.

Exercise 2: Identity

Choose the description that most closely matches what you consider your primary identity. Examine the positive and negative perceptions others may have of your identity type.

Identity Type	Positive Perceptions	Negative Perceptions
❏ Work-Focused	They are dedicated and professional.	They work too much and are detached from family.
❏ Family-Focused	They are dedicated to and protective of family.	They are rigid and self-centered.
❏ Dual-Focused	They are fully engaged, are flexible, and can do it all.	They are always busy or seem exhausted.
❏ Other-Focused	They are interesting and lead exciting lives.	They are self-centered and lack commitment to work and family.

Control

Control refers to your ability to decide when, where, and how to take care of work and family responsibilities. This is the third key factor in understanding your boundary-management style. There are three levels:

 High Boundary Control. People with a high degree of boundary control feel that they have a lot to say about how they divide their time and attention between work and family. They decide when to focus on work, when to focus on family, and when to integrate the two. They feel empowered to make decisions and to manage resulting trade-offs.

 Midlevel Boundary Control. People with a moderate degree of control feel that they have some say in how they divide their time and attention between work and family. They sometimes decide when to focus on work, when to focus on family, and when to integrate the two.

 Low Boundary Control. People with a low degree of control feel that they do not have much discretion over how they divide their time and attention between work and family. They may feel very constrained by their work schedule, family demands, or both.

How would you describe your level of boundary control?

❏ High Boundary Control

❏ Midlevel Boundary Control

❏ Low Boundary Control

With behavior and identity, there isn't one best approach, but it is better to have high or midlevel boundary control so that you feel in charge of your own schedule. This helps you meet the diverse (and often conflicting) needs or demands that you experience.

Building Your Own Approach to Boundary Management

Your approach to managing work-life boundaries is based on your combined behavior type, identity, and perceived boundary control. For example, you may be a Work Firster who is Work-Focused and has Midlevel Boundary Control. Or you could be an Integrator with a Dual-Focused Identity who has High Boundary Control. There are 60 possible combinations. All styles of behaviors and identities can potentially be associated with positive outcomes. However, only mid and high levels of boundary control are consistently associated with positive outcomes. Having low control creates obstacles to achieving positive outcomes because you may feel that the situation you are in cannot be adjusted.

Consider the following examples. Pat is Work-Focused, has High Boundary Control, and chooses to be a Work Firster in order to meet her career goals. John is Family-Focused, has Low Boundary Control, and is required to be a Work Firster because of the unusual demands of his supervisor. In this scenario, it is likely that Pat would be more satisfied with her life (both at work and at home) as compared to John. Perhaps John would be much happier if he had more boundary control and was able to use a different behavioral style (Family Firster or Separator) that would enable him to better meet his personal needs and goals. Both Pat and John could make some changes to improve their situations. Pat, however, has more options because she has a high degree of boundary control and can change the time and place she works. John has fewer options because he has little control over his work schedule.

Improving Your Boundary Management

Once you have an awareness of your own style, you can start thinking about how to make adjustments so that the positives of your boundary-management approach outweigh the negatives. The following five-step approach can help you navigate work and personal boundaries:

Step 1: Identify What Is Not Working for You

First, identify what you want to change about the way you manage work-life boundaries. What aspect of boundary management is not working for you?

Difficulty managing work-life boundaries typically centers on one or more of the following four issues: time management, boundary permeability and control, managing expectations effectively, and transitions between roles. Each of these issues is described below. As you read the descriptions, think about which, if any, relate to your situation.

Time management. Difficulty in this area highlights how little time you have to accomplish tasks in any one sphere of life. There are only 24 hours in a day, and often you may have more to do than can be accomplished in the amount of time that is available. However, you can make choices about how you allocate your time among roles. You can change how you spend your time and how you manage the trade-offs associated with those choices. The important thing to remember is to make conscious choices and to reflect on what matters most and, consequently, where you want to devote your time.

One way to tell if you have a time-management problem is to look at how you are spending your time. Use Exercise 3, Time Audit, to indicate the approximate number of hours you engage in each of the activities listed (the total should add up to 168 hours, or one week).

Exercise 3: Time Audit

In the spaces below, describe the various ways you spend your time. Examples include child care, working, civic engagements, time with friends, cleaning, commuting, eating and meal preparation, elder care, hobbies, fitness activities, home or yard maintenance, leisure, volunteering, shopping, spiritual activities, relaxing or resting, and sleeping.

Activity	Number of Hours	Percentage of Your Total Week's Time (168 hours)
Total	**168 hours**	**100%**

Adapted from Kossek & Lautsch (2008).

Exercise 3: Time Audit (continued)

Are you satisfied with how you've allocated your time? Why or why not?

_____

_____

_____

What is the impact of this time allocation on your energy levels?

_____

_____

_____

How would you like this chart to be different?

_____

_____

_____

Boundary permeability and control. Boundary permeability and control (too little separation between work and family) problems suggest that you allow yourself to be interrupted very easily. You may not focus on your personal time during nonwork hours because you are getting too many calls from work. Or it may be that you can't focus at work because you keep receiving calls from home. If you get too many interruptions, setting limits might help.

On the other hand, inviting more interruptions could make your life easier by allowing you to take care of issues as needed instead of letting them accumulate.

Intentionally exercising the degree of boundary control you have may lead to a more satisfying lifestyle. For example, workers who telecommute can benefit from dividing home and work roles so that family members understand when work occurs. One way to do this is to have a separate office space at home that is only used for working. That way, it is clear to you and others when you are at work and not open to being interrupted.

Read each of the following statements. If one or more of these apply to you, you may have a boundary-control problem:

- You constantly feel overwhelmed by requests.
- You have no time to concentrate.
- Friends, family, your boss, or coworkers complain that you are always distracted.
- You feel that you have no time for taking care of yourself.
- Your boundaries are so rigid that they don't allow for flexibility.

Managing expectations effectively. Managing expectations—your own and those of others—plays a big role in how satisfied you feel in your boundary-management strategies. If you expect to focus on parenting or work the way your parents did, consider what this will mean for you in light of all the technological and social changes that have happened between generations. Similarly, if you have family members, colleagues, a boss, or direct reports who have what you consider unrealistic expectations, discuss your perspective with them to find a solution that is mutually benefi-cial. These types of conversations, whether in your family or work life, are often difficult. However, they can lead to positive changes. Your stakeholders (a boss or a spouse, for example) may not be aware of how much stress you are experiencing and may be able to adjust their expectations or help you meet expectations in a new way. Stakeholders can often be the first to come up with strategies for substituting duties, delegating tasks, changing standards, or reducing stress. When talking with your stakeholders, take advantage of the taxonomy introduced in this guidebook. For example, it may be helpful for your stakeholders to know that you are a Separator working in an environment more suitable for an Integrator or that you need more boundary control.

Read each of the statements given below. If one or more of these items apply to you, you may have a problem managing expectations:

- You often feel surprised by what others expect of you.

- You don't really know what others expect of you. You have never discussed expectations about accessibility with your stakeholders.

- You feel that you are often disappointing someone— friends, family, your boss, or your coworkers.

- Differences around expectations trigger confrontations with others.

Transitions between roles. The transitions you make between roles pose their own challenges. However, you can use transitions to your benefit. Depending on your profile, you may want more immediate or gradual transitions. A transition ritual may help ease the transition from one role to another. For example, you can listen to upbeat or relaxing music during commuting time to gear up or unwind as you move from one role to another. You may try changing clothes to signify that you are going to work or that you are at home. Some people find it difficult to switch from a more formal, work-oriented communication style to a family style and vice versa. If your main roles require very different behaviors, focus on the transition between roles. Time buffers are another way to manage transitions. Trying to squeeze in too many things at once can cause problems, in part because it interferes with your ability to effectively transition.

If one or more of the following statements apply to you, you may have a problem with transitions:

- You consistently focus on work tasks while at home.
- You are easily distracted by nonwork issues while at work (such as surfing the Internet).
- You use a work-focused communication style while at home, or vice versa.
- You always feel as if you're working, whether you're actually at work or not.

Review the previously described ways that often trip people up when it comes to managing boundaries. What one or two areas could you improve? Could you better manage your time, better control the permeability of your boundaries, better manage expectations, or better manage transitions? Or maybe it's some other boundary problem that got you interested in this guidebook. Use Exercise 4, Areas for Improvement, to list areas where you could improve your management of boundaries.

Step 2: Learn about Boundary-Management Techniques

Learning and applying boundary-management techniques will increase the number of options you have for effectively managing boundaries. According to Kreiner, Hollensbe, and Sheep (2009) and Kossek and Lautsch (2008), several options are available to you.

Use technology to manage boundaries.

- Use technology to stay in touch with work or home.
- Use technology to separate work and home (set up separate e-mail accounts for different roles, for example), enabling you to select how and when you are contacted.

Exercise 4: Areas for Improvement

In the box below, list one or two areas where you could improve your boundary management. For example, would better management of time or expectations help you manage boundaries? Be specific in your description of the areas you choose.

Make changes based on values, needs, and other personal choices.

- Create a system for determining what is to be worked on or responded to.

- Focus on a limited number of priorities.

Create or manage physical boundaries.

- Only bring home certain types of work (administrative details, for example, rather than a full project).

- Check personal e-mails or call home only once a day and tell people outside work about your e-mail schedule.

- Have separate key rings, bags, computers, and so on for work and for home.

24

Control your time.

- Set aside blocks of time to handle work or home tasks as appropriate.
- Set aside time each day, week, or month for specific tasks.

Create time and a location for self-care.

- Choose a specific place for relaxing or for enjoying personal time.
- Set aside time to enjoy the activities you find relaxing.

Set and manage expectations.

- Indicate your boundary-management preferences to your boss, coworkers, family, and others.
- Tell significant people in your life about your various obligations so that they understand your situation.
- Explain to people who throw you off balance that you want them to interact with you differently. For example, say, "When you call me at work, I get distracted. Could you only call in cases of emergency?"

Be willing to negotiate your schedule.

- Create trades with a work or home partner (for example, say, "I'll do the grocery shopping if you take the kids to band practice").

Find a role model.

- Identify someone who manages his or her boundaries well and seek his or her advice. It might be even more helpful to ask someone with a boundary-management style similar to your own style.

Find a substitute.

- Let go of activities that do not reflect your needs or values. For example, if you do not enjoy housework but can't stand clutter, see whether you can afford to hire someone to do it for you.

- Trade tasks that you find draining or time-consuming with others who enjoy or benefit from doing them.

Pay attention to the transition between roles.

- Identify rituals that help you go from one role to another, such as listening to music, having a cup of coffee or a glass of wine, or clearing your desk.

- Change your clothes to signify to yourself and others that you have changed roles.

- Ask for some time to get organized before reentering a role.

- Leave yourself a list of tasks as you leave a particular role so that you can pick up where you left off.

Change your responsibilities or work schedule.

- Agree to take certain roles or tasks at work in exchange for more flexibility.

- Find a work schedule that supports your boundary-management efforts. For example, ask to telecommute one day a week, to switch to a part-time schedule, to use your annual leave to address a personal interest or family issue, or to delegate tasks that take time from more important work.

You may want to discuss all or some of these tactics with various stakeholders in your life to help identify the tactics that will work in your situation. You can also ask others how they manage their boundaries. Review this list, and tactics you learn from others, when aspects of work or family change and also during times of stress so that you have a relevant range of options.

Step 3: Envision a Better Life

A vision for your whole life should reflect what you want the boundaries between work and home life to be. The following advice can guide you toward that vision.

Picture the best possible way you could manage your life. What would your life be like? Frame your answer as a goal and set a specific mark you want to achieve. Then give a percentage of your chances of success. How likely is it you could achieve this goal? If the probability is 75 percent or greater, keep this image of success as a goal. If the chances for success are less than 75 percent, revise your goal to make it more achievable. Your vision of the future should be realistic. As you settle on aspects of your vision that you can probably achieve, use Exercise 5, Vision, to record them.

How will you overcome the obstacles you expect to face? Have a plan for dealing with obstacles as they arise. For example, you may set a goal to check e-mail only at designated times during the day. What will you do if someone asks you to check it more often? Know what your response will be. For example, you might reply that you only check e-mail at designated times, or you might set up a rule in your inbox to flag certain messages as high priority and requiring an answer.

With your goal in mind, use Exercise 6, Facing an Obstacle, to write down what you will do in the face of a likely obstacle.

Exercise 5: Vision

List the best possible way (or ways) you could manage your life. Then think of this list as a goal and brainstorm about the possible techniques or strategies you could employ to help you reach it.

Next, list the obstacles that could prevent you from reaching your goal (for example, commitments to work or family, expectations in your work or your personal life, habits that currently impair your management skills, and so forth).

Exercise 6: Facing an Obstacle

Use an if-then statement to indicate how you would respond to an obstacle that would prevent you from more successfully managing your time. For example, **if** you meet a likely obstacle, **then** you will respond by taking a particular action.

If _____

_____ ,

then _____

_____ .

Step 4: Get Support

Support is critical if you want to make any change. The type of support you need and where to get it are both important factors to consider. Below is a list of the general types of support people need when working on goals. You may want to consider a mix of all types of support or to focus on one or two types of support most important to you based on your situation and goals.

Emotional support. This kind of support lends encouragement to the kinds of changes you are making. For example, you might get this kind of support from a friend who is in a similar situation and can listen to and understand what you are experiencing. Your peers at work may also be good in this role.

Cognitive support. This kind of support helps you increase your knowledge about managing the boundaries between work and family. For example, a coach who knows various techniques for managing boundaries can provide you with guidance or recommend resources. You can also access e-learning resources, such as podcasts and smartphone apps, for useful information.

Political support. This kind of support helps you increase your access to organizational resources and discover opportunities related to how you manage boundaries. For example, a mentor can help you understand options for managing your work. Your boss and peers can also provide political support.

Self-support. This kind of support includes such things as changing your fitness routine or diet so you are better able to handle stress. Meditation or yoga may also be helpful additions to your support network.

Use Exercise 7, Support, to brainstorm about possible types of support you may need to improve your management of work-life boundaries.

Exercise 7: Support

Think about the four categories of support we have listed (emotional support, cognitive support, political support, and self-support). Then list below the types of support you think you need to succeed, and give specific examples. For example, if you believe you need more self-support, does that mean starting an exercise routine? Does it mean scheduling more personal time to pursue hobbies?

Step 5: Experiment and Track Your Results

Change requires focus and commitment. Make a plan and track your progress to remain accountable to yourself and your stakeholders at work and at home. Note what is working and where the pitfalls lie. Think of these plans as an experiment in boundary navigation. Experiments sometimes fail, but when they do, they yield useful information about what you can do differently. Try a variety of techniques to see which ones work the best for you and track your progress so you can refine how you manage boundaries. It can be helpful to frame your goals in terms of the benefits that matter to your stakeholders. For example, it can be important to let your boss know that you would be more productive if you were allowed to work from home one day a week.

Closing Thoughts

The boundaries between work and family have blurred, and we have to navigate them in new ways. Individuals and organizations must shift from a compartmentalized model of dividing work and personal time to a reality where boundaries are highly permeable. Developing an awareness of the three concepts central to boundary management (behaviors, identity, and control) is important so that you can understand the effects of the hyperconnectivity and constant accessibility that both produce and result from blurred boundaries. Boundaries are not fixed, and managing them takes attention. There is no one best way to handle them. Find a way that works for you and the stakeholders in your life so that you can flourish and comfortably position your work obligations in relation to all other aspects of life.

Background

This guidebook is based on research that CCL faculty conducted in partnership with Ellen Kossek between 2008 and 2012. The research had two goals: to understand how leaders manage work-life boundaries and to develop tools that would aid leaders in improving their ability to manage these boundaries. This research was conducted on alumni of CCL's open-enrollment leadership development programs and was published in *Journal of Vocational Behavior* in 2012. It also led to the creation of CCL's WorkLife Indicator assessment.

Suggested Resources

Centers for Disease Control and Prevention, National Institute for Occupational Safety and Health. (1999). *Stress...at work* (Publication No. 99-101). Retrieved from http://www.cdc.gov/niosh/docs/99-101/

Kossek, E. E., & Lautsch, B. A. (2008). *CEO of me: Creating a life that works in the flexible job age.* Upper Saddle River, NJ: Prentice Hall.

Kossek, E. E., Ruderman, M. N., Braddy, P. W., & Hannum, K. M. (2012). Work-nonwork boundary management profiles: A person-centered approach. *Journal of Vocational Behavior, 81,* 112–128.

Kossek, E. E., Ruderman, M. N., Hannum, K. M., & Braddy, P. W. (2011). WorkLife indicator: Increasing your effectiveness on and off the job [Feedback report and development planning guide]. Greensboro, NC: Center for Creative Leadership.

Kreiner, G. E., Hollensbe, E. C., & Sheep, M. L. (2009). Balancing borders and bridges: Negotiating the work-home interface via boundary work tactics. *Academy of Management Journal, 52,* 704–730.

Loehr, J., & Schwartz, T. (2004). *The power of full engagement: Managing energy, not time, is the key to high performance and personal renewal.* New York, NY: The Free Press.

Perlow, L. A. (2012). *Sleeping with your smartphone: How to break the 24/7 habit and change the way you work.* Boston, MA: Harvard Business Publishing.

Ruderman, M. N., Braddy, P. W., Hannum, K. M., & Kossek, E. E. (2011). *Making your life work: A new approach to increasing your effectiveness on and off the job.* Greensboro, NC: Center for Creative Leadership. Retrieved from www.ccl.org/leadership/pdf/research/MakingYourLifeWork.pdf

Turkle, S. (2011). *Alone together: Why we expect more from technology and less from each other.* New York, NY: Basic Books.

US Department of Labor, Bureau of Labor Statistics. (2011). *Employment characteristics of families—2010* (USDL–11–0396). Retrieved from http://www.bls.gov/news.release/archives/famee_03242011.pdf

Ordering Information

TO GET MORE INFORMATION, TO ORDER OTHER IDEAS INTO ACTION GUIDEBOOKS, OR TO FIND OUT ABOUT BULK-ORDER DISCOUNTS, PLEASE CONTACT US BY PHONE AT 336-545-2810 OR VISIT OUR ONLINE BOOKSTORE AT WWW.CCL.ORG/GUIDEBOOKS.

CPSIA information can be obtained at www.ICGtesting.com
Printed in the USA
BVOW11s1342070515

398943BV00004B/7/P